Gags for Gals

Bernadette McQuaid Murphy

authorHOUSE

AuthorHouse™ UK Ltd.
500 Avebury Boulevard
Central Milton Keynes, MK9 2BE
www.authorhouse.co.uk
Phone: 08001974150

© 2011 Bernadette McQuaid Murphy. All rights reserved.

No part of this book may be reproduced, stored in a retrieval system, or transmitted by any means without the written permission of the author.

Published by AuthorHouse 12/20/2011

ISBN: 978-1-4520-6915-9 (sc)

Any people depicted in stock imagery provided by Thinkstock are models, and such images are being used for illustrative purposes only.
Certain stock imagery © Thinkstock.

This book is printed on acid-free paper.

Because of the dynamic nature of the Internet, any web addresses or links contained in this book may have changed since publication and may no longer be valid. The views expressed in this work are solely those of the author and do not necessarily reflect the views of the publisher, and the publisher hereby disclaims any responsibility for them.

Contents

Page	Chapter
1	It's Better to be Female
2	Shorts
4	Your Know it's PMS When
5	Men are Like
6	Question Time
7	Cattitude
8	Definitions
9	Put Downs
10	Come Backs
11	Advantages of Being Male
12	Dodgy Chat Up Lines
13	Love Songs Never Recorded
15	Proverbs
16	White Lies—Gals
17	White Lies—Boys
18	Male Inventions
19	One Liners
20	Books Never Published
21	Did You Hear About
23	Things Your Mother Never Told You
24	Don't Mix Your Drinks
25	Things A Gal Would Never Say
26	Vanity in Men
27	What Annoys Gals
28	Body Talk
30	Marriage One Liners
31	Wedding Bliss
32	FAQ
33	Should He Go Or Should He Stay?
34	Tweets
36	Bride and Gloom
37	Tall Tales
39	Books for Men
40	One Liners
41	Quiz
46	Honeymoans
49	Courses For Boys
50	Cheating
51	Words Starting With Man
53	Careful Who you Date
55	Yo Boyfriend
57	Aisle Be There
59	WHY, WHY, WHY
62	Differences Between
65	Dating V Marriage
67	Pick 'n Mix
71	Smalls
73	What Men Think
76	Zodiac
78	Dumb Girls Guide
80	Seasonal Smiles
84	Howlers

Foreword

Hi Gals and welcome to Gags for Gals

Laughter pumps more oxygen into your blood and triggers the release of endorphins in much the same way as exercise, giving you that feel good factor.

Read "Gags for Gals" and share in the laughter. Ask your pals the questions at your next "gals night in" and guffaw and giggle 'till the tears stream down your face.

Are you facing a long train or bus journey? While away the miles and make the other commuters wonder what you have to smile about.

Has one of your best mates finally gone and done it? Set the date for her wedding? Is there a hen party to organise? Help the night be one to remember with these "gags for girls". Better than "truth or dare" with no hangover side effects to worry about. What are you waiting for?

Bernie

It's Better To Be Female Because:

We have better memories

Men die younger

We can put smiley faces after our messages

We never admit we're wrong!

We love a bargain

If we don't shave no one knows

We seldom have to admit our age

Lefthandedness is more common in men (we live in a right handed world)

We can increase our height with heels

Girls grow up to be women but boys grow up to be bigger boys

We can use tears as an excuse to "get away with things"

We don't fall in lust up to ten times a day

We can borrow his shirt or jacket (he could never wear ours)

We can dance with each other without being called gay

We can hug our friend without wondering if she thinks we're gay

Shorts

Sally calls her friend and tells her the mechanic says her car won't start 'cos there is a short circuit in the wiring.

Her friend who is used to getting her own way in life hesitates and then asks Sally,

"Can he not lengthen it and get it started? I've been looking forward to this shopping trip all week".

*****

"Can I not stick the wallpaper on Myself?" The elderly gentleman asked the shop assistant in the DIY store when she handed him a decorator's business card.

"Well you can, she replied but it would look better on the wall".

******

"I've come to ask you for your daughter's hand in marriage", the nervous youth told Mr. O'Connor

"Have you seen her mother?" Jack O'Connor asked looking up from his newspaper.

"Yeah, but I'd prefer to marry your daughter", he replied.

*****

A male motorist is speeding down a narrow country lane. A woman coming in the opposite direction opens her car window and screams "ASS"

The man roars back "COW"

As he reaches the bend he has to swerve to avoid two donkeys grazing on the side of the road.

*****

A lady went on a diet recommended by her friend.

She was told to eat three regular meals for two days then skip a day and repeat the pattern for two weeks. The expected weight loss was five pounds.

When she met up with her friend after two weeks her friend was amazed that she had lost a stone.

"Wow, that's amazing", her friend said. "Did you find it hard?"

"The third day was the worst," the lady said. "I thought I would drop dead".

"From hunger?" her friend asked.

"No from the skipping"

****

You know it's PMS when:

PMS: Please Myself Syndrome

Everyone you meet (even the cat) seems to have an attitude problem

The dryer has shrunk all your clothes, how else could they be so small?

You retain more water than a lake

You start counting down the days to menopause

No one else knows how to do anything right

The painkillers you bought last week are all gone

The container with the painkillers has teeth marks

You have to go to the bathroom eight times oftener than usual

When asked to pass the milk you explode – shouting, am I supposed to do everything around here?

You start asking questions that have no logical answers, example – why a round pizza is delivered in a square box?

People who don't usually agree with you are nodding to everything you say.

Men Are Like:

Shoes: too many to chose from

High Heels: easier to walk on once you get used to them

Computers: We use them but don't understand much about them

Placemats: they always show up at mealtimes

Mascara: they run at the first sign of emotion

Romance Books: They help pass the time but are easily forgettable

Pillows: Through time they tend to get "saggy"

Puppies: Fun at first but you soon get tired cleaning up after them

Cycling Helmets: useful in emergencies but not all that fashionable

A Bank Account: Without a lot of money they don't attract much interest

Sports Cars: too low and too high maintenance

Advertisements: Tell you anything to sell themselves

Cocktails: A mixture of "God Knows What"

Arithmetic: they add trouble, subtract pleasure and divide attention

Lava Lamps: enjoyable to look at but not very bright

Question Time:

How do you get rid of a man?

Tell him the only books you are interested in are cheque books.

What is the difference between a gentleman and a UFO?

There have been sightings of UFO's.

What do you call a man that's handsome, clever and sensitive?

A rumour.

What do men and parking spaces have in common?

The good ones are always taken.

What do you do if your boyfriend walks out?

Shut the door.

Why do men like intelligent women?

Opposites attract.

Where would you find a committed man?

In a mental hospital.

How do men double their money?

By folding it in half.

What did the bra say to the hat?

You go on ahead I'll give these two a lift.

What is a man's idea of a balanced diet?

A beer in each hand.

"cat-atude"

In this life I'm a woman. In my next life I'd like to come back as a cat.

When you're a cat you keep humans as slaves. As far as cats are concerned they own the whole place where they live. I could deal with that, no "probs".

I would have a sweet name like Sugar, Honey or Marmalade, nothing wrong with that.

As a cat I could sleep twenty three hours out of every twenty four, yes I could deal with that. Just need a nice soft warm surface.

When you're a "mammy cat" pregnancy only last nine weeks, and my off spring are ready to leave home at eight weeks. No college fees! Tick.

As a cat my coat won't lose it's colour or go all frizzy even when wet. So no blow-drying straightening or dyeing blonde, just a lick and I stay sleek. Purrfect.

Humans expect you to have claws and to use them, cool.

Yes, gonna be a cat!

Definitions

Divorced Male: a man who has lost 90% of his intelligence

Tears: female hydro-power

Revenge: a dish better served cold

A Gift: a man with a personality

Breast Augmentation (boob enlargement) instant sex appeal

Bachelor: a man who missed the chance to make some woman miserable

Theirs: The Inland Revenue Shower

Adult: growing out instead of up

Bra: a gal's best friend, supportive and close to the heart

Parents: Nature's Providers

Carnation: a country whose population are over reliant on cars

Ignorance I don't know

Floppy Disc: major cause of backache

Experience: mistakes

Work: the greatest thing in the world so save some for tomorrow

Simple: a man's mind

Argument: a chat that ends when one accepts that the other is right

Exercise: window shopping

Wrinkles: what other people have

Put Downs

Go evaporate

A total waste of make-up evening

Is never ok for you?

I'm out of my mind, I'll be back

What part of no don't you understand?

Back off you're invading my space

You do know how to reverse?

You wouldn't know if I was being smart with you

Watch this space, thanks

Leave it with me like for eternity

I don't do second chances

I believe in DIY (don't interfere you)

I don't need any more tragedy in my life

This is not a life changing moment

Meaningless capitalist nonsense innit

A few beads short in his mother's rosary

A cup and saucer short of a place setting

A couplet short of a sonnet

He thinks a cartoon is a song you sing in a car.

Ten seconds short of a minute

A jacket with only one sleeve.

Come Backs

Your place or mine?

Tell you what – you go to your place and I'll go to mine.

Your body is a temple!

Sorry – there are no services today.

Is this seat taken?

No and neither will this one if you sit there.

What do you say we swap positions tonight?

O.K. – You stand at the sink and I'll lie on the couch in front of the T.V.

The only reason you're dog tired is 'cos you spent the day growling at people.

What sign are you?

A clearway

Not all men are irritating – some are dead

If I throw a stick, will you leave?

Where have you been all my life?

Same place I'll always be – in your dreams.

What am I? – A magnet for losers

Excuse me I'm having a man free moment.

Stand over there, you might look better from a distance.

The Advantages of being Male: as compiled by a woman

More pay for the same job

People don't talk to your chest

Can walk into a bar alone without getting hassle

No PMS

No mid life crisis (don't mature beyond adolescence)

No danger from bag snatchers

Shorter toilet queues

Same mood all the time

Own the remote control

No expense on make-up

Hair cuts are cheaper

One case is enough to take on holiday

Can label dirty, thankless jobs as "women's work" and not have to do them

You don't care if anyone notices if you get your hair cut

You don't care if someone else is wearing the same type of clothes as you

All your shoes are comfortable (all 3 pairs)

You can be ready to go in 5 minutes

Never change your surname

Don't get over charged at the garage

Dodgy Chat Up Lines:

If you hear any of the following run……………………..

It has to be a sin to look that good

I'm here for a good time not a long time

Are you free or will it cost me

You must be Alien 'cos you're out of this world'

Are there any more like you at home

That top has to go but you can definitely stay

It's hot in here or maybe it's just you

I'm not drunk it's the effect you have on me

Can I pinch you to see if you're real

How long have you been waiting for me

You must have been made in Heaven

I wanna dance with you

I'm head over heels

I just got lost in thought about you

Top 40 Love Songs never recorded

1. Once twice three times unfaithful
2. Heart wreck hotel
3. I will woo you
4. Glam it up
5. It's Him, It's Him, It's Him
6. Infidelity
7. Imperfect Love
8. Nightmare cheater
9. Sparkler on my finger
10. Hysterics
11. Babyboom
12. Give Give Give
13. Dirty Details
14. Mr Right Now
15. The one, two and three
16. Tempted by a toy boy
17. Secret Fling
18. Highs, lows, uncertainty
19. The latest one
20. Going through the motions
21. Less is best
22. Sofa so Good
23. Duvet Disaster
24. Speak your mind
25. First Fling
26. Once, Twice, Three Times a Night
27. Marriage changes Everything
28. Stuck in a Rut
29. You can't have everything
30. Oh, No!
31. Troubleshooting
32. Insecurity

33. Up in the air
34. Clubbing
35. Pretend a little
36. Sensitivity
37. Note on her pillow
38. Seal of Approval
39. Evasive Action
40. Love makes fools of everyone

Proverbs with a Difference

Hills far away take time to reach

A stitch in time saves thread

A rolling stone stops eventually

Early to bed, early to rise makes a man tell lies

People who live in glasshouses shouldn't need a mortgage

A bird in the hand is worth seeing

Don't count your chickens until you have a calculator

The early bird catches cold

A heavy purse is hard to carry

Still waters stagnate

A shut mouth is not possible (especially if you are female)

The proof of a pudding is in the price

Two eyes are the norm

Make hay while the grass is long

Love is an emotion

It's a long road without curves

A burnt child feels pain

An apple a day signifies low pay

All that glistens catches the eye

Don't judge a book, read it

White Lies Told by Girls and what they mean

White Lie	Meaning
Love you just the way you are	Won't ask you to change yet
I'm on my way	Still in the middle of what I'm doing
It wasn't that expensive	It cost a weeks wage
I haven't seen it	I put it somewhere but can't remember
I'm fine	When you ask me ten times I'll tell you what is wrong
You're right	Be quiet
I missed your call	Chose to not answer
This isn't new I've had it for ages	Bought during my lunch hour
I wouldn't change a thing about you	I will ask you to change
I have a headache	Don't feel like it
Doesn't bother me	'course I don't like it but I need time to plan my revenge
I like your friends	Hate them all

White Lies Told by Boys and why

White Lie	**Why**
'Course you don't look fat	don't want an argument
I can fix it	want to look good in your eyes
I tried to call you	self defence
Few Beers	sounds better than eight beers
I wasn't looking, honest	afraid of being caught red handed
You'd look good in either of them	don't want the resultant hassle of choosing the wrong one
'Course I missed you	so that he won't have to explain how he spent his time while you were away
I'll never lie to you	live happily ever after fairytale
Can't remember	don't want to explain
Mad about you	sounds good
With the lads	not to worry you
Yes I'll still love you in the morning	to get you to "shut up" and let him get some sleep

Must Have Been Male Inventions

Colourless Blusher	Unleaded Pencils	Blank Recipes
Fire-proof Lighters	Non-stick Glue	Fragrance Free Perfume
Non-contact Lenses	Toothless Rakes	Fig Free Fig Rolls
Cashless ATM's	Dry Puddles	Bank Branches
Non-Removable Stationry	Clear Paint	Non flammable Tobacco
Blank Grocery Lists	Steam-less Sauna	Hands Free Handkerchief
Immobile telephones	Blank Questionnaires	Non repeatable Quotes
String-less Kites	Mite free dust	Non Operating Systems
Non-stick envelopes	Handle-less prams	Stress-free Lifestyle
Non-removable mascara	Mesh rain jackets	Open Toe Wellingtons
Suction free hoover	Air conditioning for tents	Clasp free purses
Non fastening bras	Elastic free panties	Button-less blouses
Feather paper weights	Non-grip hair clips	Silent microphones
Non swing doors	Non element electric kettle	Non rung ladders

One Liners to crack you up

The best way to become a professor is by degrees

Tax – a fine for doing well

Women who want equality with men have no ambition

Sleep like a baby – drink every three hours

Never worry about what people think – they don't do it very often

Constipated people don't give a sh**

A bargain is something you don't need offered at a great price

Take your troubles like a man – blame your wife

The best way to find the bed in a dark room is with your shin

Banks – offer finance to the people who need it least

Some people bring happiness wherever they go, others bring happiness whenever they go

Four out of five people suffer with high cholesterol does that mean one person is happy with it?

Top 20 books never published:

I Don't Know What To Make of my Husband by Cass Erole

Flawless Finish by Matt Foundation

Bit on the Side by Miss Tress

Open Air Cooking by Barbie Cue

Bad Hair Day by Frizzy Locks

Short and Sweet by Honey Moon

On A Roll by lou Paper

Beachwear by B Ikini

Cars by Robin Reliant

Crossing The River by Bridget

Aggression by D Efiant

How To Make Something Out of Nothing by Mini Skirt

Sweet and Fluffy by Candy Floss

Birth Control by E Strogen

The Writing's on the Wall by Graf Fitti

Don't Give a Hoot by Y Isowl

How To Stop Smoking by Will Power

Talking in Your Sleep by Pill O Talk

Marriage Proposals by Willie Riskit

Pricks by Rose Thorns

Did You Hear About:

The scarecrow who won an award for being outstanding in his field.

The man with the weight problem?
He couldn't wait to eat

The unfortunate bride
She didn't marry the best man

His friend with a weight problem?
His favourite food was seconds

The man who kept thinking he was a goat
He had the problem since he was a kid

The man who couldn't tell the difference between porridge and putty?
All his windows fell out

The tomato who blushed every time he saw the salad dressing

The Dad who wanted to call both his sons Ed?
He had heard that two 'eds are better than one

What the ballerina's manager did when she injured her foot?
He called the tow (toe) truck

What Hypochondriacs and fishermen have in common?
They don't have to catch anything to be happy

The 2 blood cells who loved in vein

The man in court charged with driving without due care and attention?
When asked by the judge what gear he was in, he replied, "black hoodie, white t-shirt, jeans and trainers.

The boy who told a girl he was burning with love for her?
She told him not to be a fool. (fuel)

The girl when asked during a job interview where she saw herself in 10 years time answered "in a mirror".

The stressed out toys?
They came already wound up

The man who spends more time than his wife in the bathroom?
He's a plumber

The man who ordered alphabet soup for lunch?
He wanted to read while he ate

The man who ate a currant scone before going sailing?
So if his boat sank the current (currant) would bring him ashore

The man who stole a truck full of prunes?
He's been on the run ever since

The florist who had two children?
One is a budding genius and the other is a blooming fool

The musical ghost?
Sings haunting melodies

The woman who injured her back doing a good deed?
One day when out shopping she came across a man sitting on the pavement who asked her for a helping hand.

Bending over him she grasped him by the arm and tried to haul him to his feet

The new bride who went to the greengrocers every day 'cos she new her husband would ask every evening for turnip and lettuce

The man who fitted all the windows of the house with blinds 'cos he didn't like seeing his wife doing heavy physical work in the garden.

The child who answered salt, pepper, vinegar and tomato ketchup when the teacher asked him to name the four seasons.

10 Things Your Mother Never Told You

Don't date men shorter than yourself – will see you as a mother figure and never sweep you off your feet.

Three good friends to see you through any crisis: feigned illness, sleepiness and headaches.

The one holding your hand may not be the one holding your heart.

Goldfish, mice, plants etc: they all die and so do we.

Practise doing the crossword in the daily paper 'cos like men they have different levels of difficulty and you're never 100% sure you've got the right answer.

The "love rat" gene does exist.

No "wild time" when you're young can cause problems in your thirties.

Men only dress up for weddings and funerals

Many men are intent in chasing after women who avoid them, just as many dogs are intent in chasing after cars that elude them.

Gals Don't mix your drinks:

What a waste of hours getting all dolled up if you're going to spend the night wasted.

Everyone has a lethal alcoholic cocktail that releases the beast within, when you discover yours shun it.

Things gals do when they've had one too many:

Say "oh my God this is my favourite song ever" to every track that's played.

They wanna dance, dance, dance with everybody – well anybody.

Blame their shoes when balancing becomes a problem.

Start a deep meaningful conversation with the lad they dismissed as a loser earlier.

Giggle uncontrollably at everything.

No longer care that their make-up is streaky

Repeat some unknown word over and over.

Don't know what they are drinking as they can no longer taste it.

Remember gals alcohol isn't the answer when you can't remember the question!

Things a gal would never say:

I'm wrong

Oh look that girl's top is like mine I must congratulate her on her good taste.

Don't worry about getting me something for Valentines' day, treat yourself and your mates instead.

I can't stand shopping

You sure you've had enough to drink?

I'm neurotic

Ask your mates to come along.

I will never complain again

Go ahead and keep staring at every woman that passes by, I don't mind.

Lets just sit here in silence.

I know how to put this together I don't need the instructions.

Those trousers don't make you look fat, I mean – how could they?

She's more a has been than a wannabe

She would argue with a recipe

You can't have everything

I do create my own reality

Women weren't put on this earth to be happy.

And They Say Gals Are Vain:

A bald man once tattooed rabbits on his head 'cos from a distance they looked like hares.

There are few magazines for men, because they think they know it all

Don't believe in an official "me-time"

Don't change their surname

Men suck in their tummies every time they see an attractive lady to appear taller, more masculine or just to hide the results of months of take-aways

Men drive big cars

Don't do guilt

They claim they can multi-task because they watch T.V. and have breakfast at the same time.

They believe they are fault free

If you try to point out their faults they dismiss it as nagging

Men can fake a whole relationship

They never read instruction leaflets

They never feel the need to ask for directions

Will never admit to being wrong

10 Things That Annoy Us Gals

People who chew on pens that they have borrowed

Boys who make up stories to make themselves sound impressive

Those who laugh loudest at their own jokes

When you order chips and someone eats half of them even though they said they weren't hungry

People who talk about their connections (the name dropping brigade gals)

Generalizations by boys, like about blonde gals

Gals who say certain boys fancy them when truth is they aren't vaguely interested (come on now gals)

Interruptions when we're in full flow with a good story

Having to decide between the silver or the purple killer heels when we know we have things at home that would go with either

Inadequate signposts (we have lots on our minds so make it obvious for us)

Body Talk: A Guide To What His Body Is Saying:

Body language, the oldest human language can be misleading, the following are an indication of what he is thinking.

If he invites you round and plays easy to listen to music with dim lights or candlelight: a romantic and sensitive lad.

Soft Kisses: no gals it doesn't mean that he's a bit soft! More like he's sweet, a gentleman, this one really likes you.

Eye Contact: this is a good sign, he's ready to connect with you. Watch out though if he narrows his eyes, (dogs do this, the four legged ones) it shows dislike.

Excessive hand movements means he is lying.

If he is attracted to you he will play with his ear lobe and his feet will point in your direction.

If he adopts a "cowboy stance" standing with his legs apart and the hands on the hips or thumbs in the belt with fingers pointing down towards the genital area he is giving a macho display.

Smoothing the hair is a male version of the hair flick and is a preening gesture.

Sleeping Position

Foetal: insecure, a sensitive vulnerable soul, bless him.

Pillow hugging: this one will need reassurance that you care.

Facedown on his stomach: tread carefully here, can signify he is energetic and outgoing but also could be that he is a little bit controlling.

Body Talk: A Guide to What You Gals are Saying:

Girls use signals which play up their "girlness" by drawing attention to the softest parts of the body, cleavage, neck, wrists and genitals.

The Eyes: when a girl wants to attract a man she catches his eye and then quickly looks away or down, she does this a few times.

Doe-eyes: this is when the gal glances at the man slightly sideways or through lowered eyelashes while keeping the head and chin down. This look is very appealing to the boys because you are saying "I'm interested" but with a child-like shyness.

The hair flick: bouncy healthy looking hair is attractive, when a gal flicks her hair away from her face or runs her fingers through it she is inviting the boy to approach.

Licking the lips: another invitation to the boy to approach. Girls lips are bigger than boys (usually) so licking them draws attention to her femaleness. Colouring the lips with gloss or lippy attract the boys to take a second look.

Fake Smiles: gals give more fake smiles than boys! Real smiles always start in the eyes, fake smiles are made only with your mouth. Fake smiles usually leave the face slower than a real smile.

Marriage One Liners

Married men live longer

The secret to a happy marriage remains a secret

The two times a man doesn't understand a woman is before marriage and after marriage

He may seem sweet and lovely on the day but remember he's a man

The woman always has the last word in an argument

Don't judge each other by your relations

Don't imagine you can change him – unless his is in nappies

Tie-straightening is a giveaway that he fancies who he is talking to

Don't let his mind wander, it's too small to be out on it's own

Men are not as fashion conscious as women

Men are like photo-copiers, necessary for reproduction

Teach your son to cut his own wood, it will keep him twice as warm

Arguments wouldn't last long if the fault is one sided

Everything has an ending

Wedded Bliss:

Husband and wife have been married twenty two years. Getting ready one Friday night to attend husband's Christmas work party. Husband shouts out to wife,
"Are you ready yet"? she shouts back,
"Didn't I tell you half an hour ago I'd be down in a minute".

A wife got revenge on her work shy husband after he passed away, she had him cremated and put his ashes in an egg timer.

Husband looked at wife after trying for half an hour to put a flat pack make-up table together.
"No, can't do it", he told her.
"What"? his wife asked in disbelief grabbing the instructions. "Any ten year old could do it", she told him after scrutinising the sheet for a few minutes.
"NO wonder I can't do it then, sure I'm nearly sixty"

FAQ

Frequently asked questions by gals:

When Shopping:

Can I fit into this?

Can I afford it?

Why is the lighting here so bad?

Do you have these in pink? Blue? Silver?

Do I need another pair?

What have I at home to match?

To Boys:

Do you love me?
How much?
Are you sure?
What are you thinking?
Is she prettier than me?
Where were you?
To their Friends?
Do I look fat in this?
Should I dump him?
So?
What do you think?
How much?
Is it fattening?

Frequently asked questions by boys:

When Shopping:

Do I need it?

How much?

To Gals:

What?
Does it matter?
Where?
Why not?
Your place or mine?

To their Friends?
What was the score?
What you havin?
Did you see it?
Who was there?
How much?

Should he go or should he stay?

Go	**Stay**
If he is commitment shy then he goes	If his mission is not to get but to give he stays
Wasted most of the time, lose him	Your friends like him, keep him
Talks of love at first sight, tread carefully	Your Mum likes him, he stays
Avoids discussing "us" let him go	Goes shopping with you, tick!
Long silences between you, the elbow!	Shared interests, keep an open mind!
Refuses to cook or clean up after self forget him	Makes tea, toast, use microwave, has potential
Only thinks with the contents of his Boxers, leave him to own devices	Avid watcher of Discovery channel? check out his bookshelves
A fan of the "no effort" philosophy have no expectations and you will definitely not be disappointed	Goes to great lengths good, encourage him all the way to look good, smell

Two lads tweet on twitter:

1st Lad: She has legs like matchsticks though

2nd Lad: Correction mate, they look like sticks but they don't match

1st Lad: She's so dumb, she rang my home phone number the other day and when I answered do you know what she asked me?

2nd Lad: Knowing her it could be anything

1st Lad: She said, is that you Pete? Who the f… did she think it would be

2nd Lad: Well she is blonde Pete, what do you expect?

1st Lad: It was love at first sight man

2nd Lad: Yeah!

1st Lad: Until I took a second look

1st Lad: Love is like a photograph

2nd Lad: 'cos it takes time to develop, yeah?

1st Lad: Sort of but more like it needs darkness to develop

2nd Lad: Good one mate, good one

Two Gals Tweet on Twitter

1st Gal: We like create life, we give life and like we sustain life

2nd Gal: Absolutely, while they're more like laxatives, "shit stirrers" know what I mean

1st Gal: Max is like a rollercoaster

2nd Gal: Wow! What do you mean

1st Gal: Whenever I think about him I feel like throwing up

2nd Gal: Seriously like, wow!

1st Gal: I want to break up with Rob, what should I say?

2nd Gal: Tell him you love him, want to marry him and have six children. You won't see him for dust.

1st Gal: It makes me livid when they presume that they are the only ones with a sense of humour.

2nd Gal: I know Jackie, I know. To be honest the very fact that us girls have husbands is proof that we can take a joke.

Bride and Gloom:

Now Gals don't marry for money, a loan from a financial institution is cheaper. If you can afford to pay back extra every month you will be able to get out of it quicker.

What are you looking for in a husband?

If you want someone who will make you laugh, spend time with you and stay home at night then you should seriously consider getting yourself a telly instead. The advantage to this is you can switch it off when you're done and know it will be where you left it the next morning.

People compare marriage to a guitar. Enjoyable but has strings that goes with it.

Others will tell you compromise is important in a marriage. I'm not sure what they mean exactly but I suppose if he admits he does wrong you can compromise by agreeing with him.

In the first two years of marriage he speaks and she listens.
In the next two years she speaks and he listens.
In years five and six both of them speak and none of them listen.
After that neither of them speaks to each other.

Marriage is said to be like a bath. Nice at first but the longer you stay in it the colder it gets.

In a marriage one person is always right and the other person is the husband.

Be careful gals that when you fell head over heels in love that you weren't tripped.

Remember that the word trouble starts with "t" and so does tyres, testicles and trapped.

Many children have imaginary friends which is quite acceptable just think of the advantages of imaginary husbands.

Tall Tales:

There once was two ladies called Sally and Jenny. They died on the same day and met in heaven.

"Hi", Sally said to Jenny. "My name is Sally".

"Hi Sally" Jenny replied. "I'm Jenny".

"Nice to meet you Jenny. You're very young, do you mind if I ask you how you died"? Sally asked.

"I froze to death", Jenny said matter of factly.

"Froze to death, you poor thing, that must have been awful".

"Well, to be honest I don't remember that much about it", Jenny told her before asking. "What about yourself, what happened to you"?

"I died from a massive heart attack", Sylvia told her.

"Oh, but you're so slim and healthy looking".

"I was in such a panic you see. I hurried home from work early 'cos I thought my husband was having an affair and I wanted to catch him at it. But when I got home I found him sitting in the kitchen reading the newspaper and drinking a cup of tea. So I raced around the house looking to see if she was hiding anywhere. I searched upstairs and downstairs, I even ran to the bottom of the garden and back looking under the hedging to see if I could find her. As I went in the back door I collapsed and died".

"Too bad you didn't look in the freezer", Jenny said quietly. "If you had we'd both be still alive.

Santa, the tooth fairy, a kind handsome man and a drunk man are walking together in the Cathedral car park.

A sudden gust of wind blows a 100 euro note into their path. Which of them gets the note?

The drunk man. Why? ('cos the other 3 don't really exist).

Books for men written by gals:

How To Accept Success in Women

Dish-washing for Dummies

The 3 Keys to Better Hearing

How To Dig a Hole Big Enough to Get Into

Self-Care Manual for Boys

Beating the Follicle Challenge

Getting Things Done in 2 Easy Steps

The Armchair Referee

How To Replace a Loo Roll in Thirty Seconds

What To Do With Wet Towels

On the Move

Why Bigger is Not Better

Living In Peace

Wasted Days and Wasted Nights Add Up

Non Stressful Shopping

Understanding No

The Effects of long term Staring on the Eyes

How To Return Phone Calls

Listening Skills for Men

100 Things To Do Before You Marry

The Unfamiliar Territory of Commitment

The 3S's: Sincerity, Sensitivity & Sensibility

Honesty – The Best Policy – Honestly

Giggle inducing one liners:

Some people (men) appear bright until they speak 'cos light travels faster than sound

Gals generally were known to be indecisive now I'm not sure

Rush hour is the name given to the time of day when traffic is at its' slowest

The first half of a persons life is ruled by parents and the second half by their children

The 3 little words to humiliate any man are "hold my bag"

Everyone complains about the cost of living yet no one is willing to give it up

If you think nobody cares just stop paying your bills for a few months

Gals only ever learn how to truly swear when they learn to drive

Never punch anyone with glasses, your fist is more effective

Worrying works, most of the things we worry about never happen

Quiz Time Gals:

Two points for each correct answer, there are five rounds of five questions.
May the best gal win!!

Round 1

Question 1
What am I:
He chose me carefully. Held me tight. Took me home. Took off my top and put his lips on mine?

Answer
A bottle of wine.

Question 2
How do you get over from a lover?

Answer
Take away the letter "L"

Question 3
Why do gals get paid les than men?

Answer
'Cos our work is never done'

Question 4
Why did the psychic cross the road?

Answer
To get to the other side

Question 5
The average bed contains how many dust mites?
10,000 (b) 2,000 (c) 100

Answer
10,000. Yes, really!!

Round 2.

Question 1
What falls but never breaks?

Answer
Night

Question 2
What provides your daily intake of calories in one go?

Answer
A box of choices (I swear)

Question 3
What does stressed give if spelled backwards?

Answer
Desserts

Question 4
Do you consume more calories when dining out with (a) men, (b) other women, (c) is it the same?

Answer
(b) women, honestly (and the moral of this is……)

Question 5
Can you touch your toes?
yes, (b) can't see my toes, (c) can touch my ankles

Answer
Score 1 point for answer c, 2 points for answer a, 0 points for answer b.

How are you getting on? Good!
Next round

Round 3 (How well do you know your men?)

Question 1
How does a man plan for the future?

Answer
He buys enough beer for the whole week-end.

Question 2
How is a man like a beer bottle?

Answer
They are both empty from the neck up.

Quesstion 3
What do you give a man that has everything?

Answer
A gal to show him how to use it.

Question 4
How does a man get regular exercise?

Answer
By constantly pushing his luck.

Question 5
Why is divorce so expensive?

Answer
.cos it's worth its weight in gold.

Round 4

Question 1
What am I?
My maker doesn't want me. My buyer doesn't use me. My user never sees me.

Answer
A coffin

Question 2
What is everyone in the world doing at the same time?

Answer
Growing old

Question 3
How many birthdays does the average person have?

Answer
One

Question 4
What animals gives us catgut?

Answer
Sheep and horses (Who said cat?)

Question 5
How many months have twenty eight days?

Answer
12 (Yes they all do – sorry trick question)

Not doing so well – never mind you
Can make up lost ground in the final round

Round 5 True or False, c'mon gals you can catch up here and get a clear round

Question 1
When awake the brain generates enough energy to work a light bulb

Answer
True (25 watts apparently)

Question 2
12 out of 10 people are bad at maths

Answer
False (you can't get 12 out of ten

Question 3
Love potions exist naturally within everyone

Answer
True (2 brain chemicals called dopamine and serotonin) (Was that a guess?)

Question 4
Pepsi Cola was invented by Dr. Pemberton in 1866 as a cure for hangovers

Answer
True

Question 5
65% of our bodies is water

Answer
True

And the results are in
Five rounds of five questions with two points per correct question
If you scored

40 – 50: Hey bright spark- congratulations! No fooling you. Seriously though this is a fantastic result. Give yourself a pat on the back for your high achievement.

30 – 40: Well done you! You seem to be one of those who are always up for it- a mental challenge that is. What did you think I meant?

20 – 30: You are on the right track! A little room for improvement though, would you agree? A slight concentration problem with not enough attention to detail perhaps.

Under 20: This is not like you! A one off I'm sure. Don't fret better luck next time. You were having an off day – I understand! It's not all bad 'cos the only way from here is up.

Honeymoans:

Jason and Kelly had just got married and had a lavish reception with 300 guests, that night they retired to the honeymoon suite. After an hour of kissing and cuddling Jason asked.
"Do you object to making love?"
"That's something I have never done before" Kelly answered
"Made love" Jason asked in surprise.
Kelly burst out laughing
"No you fool, objected"

"What's your definition of marriage then" Pam asked Tommy, her husband of forty eight hours
Tom paused thinking deeply before saying.
"A game of poker I suppose"
"Poker" asked Pam "How on earth could marriahe be like poker"
"Well it starts with holding hands and there's a good chance it will end in financial ruin

"A honeymoon" explained twice married Liz should be like a mini-skirt short enough to make them wonder but not too revealing

"How will I know when the honeymoon period is over?" Beth asked her Auntie.
When he starts ringing to say he will be late home and you start leaving a message on the answer-phone to say his dinner is in the oven.

Twenty year old newly married Rose rang her mother in tears.
"Whats wrong love" her mother asked
"I hate him Mum, he keeps using all these awful four letter words to me" Rose sobbed
"Like what love"
"Cook, iron, dust, wash."

Definitions of wife
Wash, iron, fetch, endure!
Willingly fake enjoyment!
Wasn't I fooled easily!
Wacky Institute of Further Education

Things not to say on Honeymoon

Best rule is if in doubt keep quiet

Is this your first time?
Yeah today

Your almost as good as my ex
My cat usually sleeps there

I'm tired
I have a headache

I'll just check with the girls

Lena and Pete get married having met at the Christmas party for older members of the community. On the night of their honeymoan Lena asks:

Pete, where are your new dentures? and he replies
I'm leaving them out 'till I get used to wearing them.

Dawn and Dave get married and go on a ten day honeymoan to an isolated country cottage. It rains every day and night while they are there. On the ninth night cuddled up in bed listening to the rain dancing off the roof they decide to ask each other "Knock Knock" jokes. Dave starts with "Knock Knock" Who's there?
 Nicholas
Nicholas who? Asks Dawn
Nicholas girls shouldn't climb trees

A teacher of English was encouraging her class of twelve year olds to write a mixture of long and short sentences in their essays to make their writing more interesting. She asked one twelve year old, 'Kenny will you write an example of a long sentence on the board please". Kenny strutted up to the board and wrote just one word "marriage".

Further Education Courses for the Boys:

Listening Skills
Ironing for Pleasure
Beating Remote Control Dependence
Understanding Girls Beginners, Intermediate, Advanced
Asking For Directions, how, why and when
Avoiding Temptation, the Complete Guide in six easy lessons
Sensitivity Explained
Finding The Right Words, a series of workshops
Taking care of your "smalls"
Caring For the Dishes
The Importance of Ringing Home
Cleaning Equipment Explained

Further Education Courses for the Girls:

How To Get Exactly What You Want From The Man In Your Life:
What to Do When He Messes Up
The Art of Faking
You're sitting On a Gold Mine How to Use It to Your Extreme Advantage:
Beginners
Intermediate
Advanced
Decorating the Spare Bedroom
Keeping Dinners Warm
Pretend Gardening
Training Your Nearest and Dearest in Household Care
How to Find a Good Mechanic
Plausible Excuses and When to Use Them
Dressing your man on a Budget
How best to store Shoes

Some thoughts on why men cheat: nobody really knows why not even men themselves!

Women usually go through a list of possible reasons in their head trying to work out why?

Some men cheat
Some do it well
Some not so well!

Gals have a tendency to get all excited about nothing and marry him
Men cheat 'cos
They are short term thinkers
Only moving objects get their attention
They are always on the look-out for two for one deals
They never mature so they like to play
They cheat at cards so to them it's a natural progression
Nothing lasts forever is their philosophy for life
They are natural risk takers
They see themselves as hunter gatherers
Like dogs and cats they love the thrill of the chase
And finally just because they can!

A list gals that starts with men, man, guy, his/hys, read it carefully and give it sufficient thought!

Menace
Menagerie (a small zoo)
Mendacious (lying)
Menial
Menopause
Menstruate
Mental
Manacle (shackle for the wrist or ankle)
Management
Mandatory (compulsory)
Mandrake (a poisonous plant0
Mangle (clothes dryer)
Manful (brave)
Manhandle
Mange (skin disease of dogs)
Manhole
Manhood
Mania
Manipulate
Manliness
Manoeuvre (a crafty plan)
Manpower
Manslaughter
Manure
Guy Fawkes
Gynecologist
His
Hiss (sign of disapproval)

History (most of them come with a history)
Histrionic (acting)
Hysterical
Hysterics
Hysterectomy

      ****

Her on the other hand appears in
Herculean (hero of great strength)
Heroine and
Hero Heron
Hereditary
Heretic (holder of an opinion not generally accepted as right and true)
She in:
Sheer
Sheen
Sheath (close fitting cover e.g. condom)
Sheep (timid beast)
Sheet
Sheikh   Shelter (protection against harm)

Careful who you date gals:

If you date:
A driver: you might get taken for a ride
A bin-man: he may dump you
A carpet fitter: could walk all over you
A policeman: will be tempted to cuff you
A telephone engineer: could turn out to be a phoney
A comedian: will make a joke of you
A musician: would play you along
A golfer: sure to put you in the bunker
An electrician: sparks will fly
A history teacher: you would become a thing of the past
A jogger: tempted to give you the run around
A businessman: might see you as a liability
An unemployed man: you will have to keep working for his benefit
A train driver: will always keep track of you
A footballer: will be looking to score straight away

Gals if you're not sure about dating a man perhaps you would consider a horse or a dog. To help you in your decision I have listed the advantages of both.

A Horse:	**A Dog:**
There are no in-laws	His favourite drink is water
They don't look at T.V.	Doesn't have a surname that you will be expected to use
Delighted to see you if you have an apple or carrot	Always happy to see you
Accept restraint	Faithful
Don't need any laundry doing	Doesn't watch T.V.
Prefer to stay outdoors	Won't bring his mates around
If it doesn't work out you can sell them	You won't have to dress up to go out with him/her
Don't like pubs	Doesn't use toilet roll
Don't mess up	Will only chase four legged bitches
Can be trained to jump	Prefers to sleep at the end of the bed
Don't boast to their friends	Will not argue with you
Will not stare at other girls	Usually comes to you when called

Yo Boyfriend So Old

Yo boyfriend so old he went to pre-school with Ella Fitzgerald.
Yo boyfriend so old he has a free travel pass
Yo boyfriend so old he passed his driving test in a horse and cart
Yo boyfriend so old when he was young rainbows were black and white
Yo boyfriend so old he had more candles than cake on his last birthday
Yo boyfriend so old he still has his ration book
Yo boyfriend so old he left his wallet at the Last Supper
Yo boyfriend so old he was one of the crew who installed the first parking meter
Yo boyfriend so old he remembers when coco-cola was sold as a medicine
Yo boyfriend so old he was one of the first to use the three coloured traffic lights

Yo Boyfriend So Stupid

Yo boyfriend so stupid he got hit by a parked car.

Yo boyfriend so stupid he was born on January first and he can't remember his birthday.

Yo boyfriend so stupid his waist is bigger than his I.Q.

Yo boyfriend so stupid he studied for a blood test.

Yo boyfriend so stupid he put when I can as his sex on an application form.

Yo boyfriend so stupid he was up all night wondering why birds never smile.

Yo boyfriend so stupid he failed a questionnaire.

Yo boyfriend so stupid he thinks PMT is an abbreviation for mobile telephone.

Yo boyfriend so stupid he refused to take a shower in case someone else might want it.

Yo boyfriend so stupid he returned a packet of polo mints for a refund because parts of them were missing.

Aisle Be There: Some more marriage funnies gals:

Husband: I read in the paper today that women use twice as many words in a day than men.

Wife: That's because we have to repeat everything we say to men.
Husband: What?

****

Husband: I don't know why you wear a bra, you have nothing to put in it.

Wife: You wear underpants, don't you?

****

Wife: If you want breakfast in bed you better sleep in the kitchen.

****

Coffee, chocolate, husbands – some things are just better rich!

****

Man's definition of marriage: an expensive way of getting your clothes washed.

****

A couple in their late eighties was celebrating their sixtieth wedding anniversary. A reporter from the local newspaper asked them what the secret was to such a long marriage. "Both of us are hard of hearing, I suppose that helped," the wife replied.

****

Wife: How would you feed if it was no longer just the two of us, you know if we became three?
Husband: That's great, when?
Wife: This weekend, my mother's coming to stay.

****

Husband: When I'm gone I bet you won't find another man like me.
Wife: Why would I want another one like you?

****

Husband: I'll make you the happiest woman in the world.

Wife: Where are you off to?

****

Wife: Do these jeans make my bum look like the side of the house?

Husband: No, sure our house isn't blue.

****

Wife: What's on the T.V. tonight love?

Husband: Not sure but it looks like dust.

****

Husband: How is the driving coming along?

Wife: I didn't think I was making any progress at all but today when I came back from the supermarket I got a note on my windscreen saying parking fine.

WHY, WHY, WHY:

Why are blonde jokes so short?

So men can read them in one go, understand and remember them.

****

Jack spent 3 days in hospital. When discharged he was totally healthy but couldn't walk.
Why?
Jack was only 3 days old.

****

Why don't men die in their sleep?

'Cos they can't do two things at once

****

Why is psychoanalysis quicker for men?

They don't need to revisit their childhood because they're already there.

****

Why are men like a food processor?

You think you need one, but you're not quite sure why.

****

Why did the man call his dog sandwich?

Because he was a half-bred.

****

Why did the man wear his shirt in the shower?

Because the label said wash and wear.

****

Why did the bald man go outside?

Because he wanted to get some fresh hair.

****

Why do men whistle when they are on the toilet?

So that they will know which end to wipe.

****

Why did the washing machine laugh?

'Cos it was taking the piss out of the pants.

****

Why do female black widow spiders kill the males after mating?

To prevent the snoring which is sure to start.

****

Why do men propose marriage?

To make it illegal for you to marry someone else.

****

Why did the man think he couldn't draw his breath?

Because he was never very good at art.

****

Why did the man take his bike to bed?

He didn't want to walk in his sleep.

****

Why did the man wear two pairs of trousers when playing golf?

In case he got a hole in one.

****

Why did the man plough his field with a steam roller?

He wanted to grow mash potato.

Differences between:

A chest infection and a man: while both can make you feel weak, the chest infection will go away with treatment.

****

Rubbish and men: they both cost but when you put out the rubbish it stays out.

****

An untidy room and a man: they both look awful but you can tidy up the room.

****

Hangovers and men: both cause suffering but at least with the hangover you've had a good time.

****

Babies and men: both need a lot of attention but babies become more independent as they get older.

****

Books and men: while neither should be judged by their outside covers, the books can be passed on to others easily.

****

Horses and men: both 'nuzzle' at your hair but horses respond to a click of the tongue.

****

Men and cheese: while both have a distinctive smell, cheese matures.

****

The weather and men: you can't change either of them but you get sunny spells of weather.

****

Men and horoscopes: they both tell you what to do but the horoscopes are funny.

****

Men and chairs: both have a role in life but the chair will support you.

****

Men and water: while they are both tasteless the water is refreshing.

****

Men and popcorn: popcorn is tasty even though like men it will only satisfy you for a little while.

****

Men and Tamagotchis (electronic pets): both require attention but Tamagotchis don't need to be house trained.

****

Men and varicose veins: walking each day will improve the tone of the veins and surgery will remove them.

****

Men and shampoo: the wrong shampoo like the wrong man can be a source of irritation but a good shampoo is caring.

Boys change between the dating stage and marriage; here are some of the differences:

Dating	V's	M a r r i a g e
He will wine and dine you.		He brings home beer and expects a cooked dinner.
He's mad about you.		He's mad at you.
There is chemistry between you.		There is history between you
You discuss everything		He develops a hearing problem.
He loves your curves.		He calls you fat.
He's in love with you.		He's in love with himself.
Finds your habits cute.		Your habits irritate him.
Asks at dinner: is that all you're having?		Suggests you should have salad.
Holds your hand.		Holds the remote.
Always happy to see you coming.		Happy to see you go.
Calls you by name or pet name.		Calls you 'she' 'you' and 'her'
You are the sunshine of his life.		You are the cloud before the rain.

Dating V's	**Marriage**
Laughs at your jokes.	You have to laugh at his.
Happy to dine by candlelight	Only thinks about dining by candlelight if there is a power cut.
Gives you compliments.	Never notices a new hairstyle.
Gives choccies and flowers to impress.	Gives choccies and flowers 'cos he's messed up.
Happy to wait ages for you.	Can't wait for a minute.
Calls you at least once a day.	Calls you only when he wants something.
Accepts that you have male friends.	Thinks any man who talks to you wants you.
Makes an effort with your Mum.	Keeps out of her path.
Tolerates your girlfriends.	Sarcastic with and about your girlfriends.
Buys deodorants etc and uses them lavishly.	Uses yours if at all.
Cuddles on the couch.	Sleeps on the couch.
Enjoys the Sound of Music.	Enjoys the Sound of Silence.

Pick 'n Mix:

Gals, the next four pages have a mixture of jokes and thought provoking statements, enjoy!

Equality:
We have a better chance of getting equality with the boys when we start walking down the street follicley challenged, with a beer gut and still think we're God's gift.

The perfect man:
If your friend boasts that she has found "the perfect man" be content in the knowledge that nobody is perfect. So logically this man must be a nobody!

Glasses:
For those gals who wear glasses you have the advantage that if you want your man to see things your way; just lend him your glasses.

Shoes:
If the shoe fits gals buy them in every available colour.

Forget your troubles – wear tight shoes.

Women Drivers:
Definition:
Doesn't speed, tailgate, rev inappropriately, have noisy smoky exhausts, swear or make obscene gestures.

Love rats are like your appendix, can be troublesome and painful but when it's gone you realise you didn't need it.

Cathy and Tom separated on religious differences – he thought he was God and she didn't.

If another gal swipes your boyfriend/hubby, the best revenge is to let her keep him.

In this life gals you will meet three types of men:

Sensitive: 2%
Trustworthy: 4%
The others: 94%

When us gals get married we're looking for the 3 p's, pampering, passionate, and presentable but what we get are the 100 un's, I will only list 10 to be fair!
unimaginative, uncanny, unyielding, unwilling, unsteady, unreasonable, untidy, ungallant, uncovered and unconcerned.

Husband and Wife 10 months after wedding:

Husband: I read in a newspaper article today that the best way to keep your wedding ring in pristine condition is to soak it regularly in warm dishwater.

Wife: Written by a man no doubt.

Two men talking:

1st man: Breakfast seems to take forever in our house, Moira walks miles taking things out one by one and putting them on the table.

2nd man: It was the same in ours until I suggested she do it differently. Now it takes about five minutes.

1st man: Oh! What changed?

2nd man: She stays in bed now and makes me do it.

Two single men talking:

1st man: I have two cookbooks but I don't use them.

2nd man: Why not?

1st man: Well I did try but every page I opened started with "take a clean dish", and I couldn't continue.

Bride and Groom seventy two hours before the Wedding:

Him: when we are married I will share the housework equally with you.

Her: Great, what parts of it will you do?

Him: I was thinking if you do the cooking, the cleaning, the washing, the dishes, the hovering and the gardening, I will do the rest.

Two months after the wedding husband and wife are having their 'first' row when he arrives home the 'worst for wear' in the early hours of the morning.

Wife: Where were you 'till this hour?

Husband: Playing golf with the lads love.

Wife: 'Till three o'clock in the morning. What the hell were you using? Night Clubs?

Two Wives talking:

1st Wife: Husbands are like hoovers you know Cathy.

2nd Wife: Why Tina?

1st Wife: Well once you get used to them you can push them around easily enough.

What did one light bulb say to the other light bulb?

I love you a whole watt.

What did the light bulb say to the switch?
You turn me on.

What did the candle say to the match?
You're the light of my life.

What did the thunder say to the lightning?
Are we there yet?

Now gals some doctor, doctor jokes:

Doctor, Doctor I think I'm a dog
Have a seat on the couch and we'll discuss it
But doctor, I'm not allowed up on the couch.

Doctor, Doctor I think I'm a spoon
OK sit down there and don't stir.

Doctor, Doctor I keep taking things that aren't mine
Now you have to try and avoid the temptation but if you can't I need a special piece of jewellery for my wife's fiftieth birthday.

Hilarious Smalls:

The small ads gals can be the source of great gags. The next two pages have a selection, some of which did occur due to typo's I presume.

Cars For Sale:
Mercedes 240 diesel, lonely condition (lovely)
'04 Megane Hunchback (hatchback)

Lonely Hearts:
Vicious (vivacious) lively lady 38 seeks similar male.
56 year old window (widow) would like to meet gentleman for friendship.
Lady mid forties likes reading and talking.

Summer Sale:
Men's skirts (shirts) from €9.50
Bargain Rain (rail) suits from €99.00

On the Menu:
Worm (warm) apple pie and cream
Pupperoni pizza

Insulation for:
Patio doors, sun rooms and torches (porches)
Get (gel) Nails for €40.00

Available:
Bandage (Band) available for New Year's Eve

Wanted:
Old things by serious collector

Handy man for Summer months

Cleaner (cleaning) lady wanted

7 nights Half-Bored (board) in 3star hotel.

Good quality toe (top) soil for sale.

For Sale: Hand (sand) small or big loads.

Female with preferences (references) looking for work as cleaner/carer.

Bar and wasting (waiting) staff required.

For Sale: Ride on Dawnmower (lawn)

Car praying (spraying) available.

Swinging (singing) lessons available in your home.

Party Packages include party fool (food)

Men (hen) parties and groups

6 drawer dressing table oaf (oak)

Mobile wedding (welding) available.

Does your dog 'pull' when walking? 4 week intensive obedience classes available.

More Cars For Sale:

Honda Civic, red alloy wheels, few (new) tyres

Toyota Avensis '01 diesel saloon slow (low) mileage

Renault Clio taxed and rested (tested)

Nissan Micra one lazy (lady) owner

Opel Corsa, no reasonable offering (offer)

Subaru 2000 1.6 L, alloys front and back spoiled (spoiler)

Sales Rep required:

Duties include to melt (meet) with customers

Commis waiter/waitress needed, some knowledge of food and wind (wine) desirable.

What Men Think

Labour Pains are:	(feeling) sore from working too hard.
Abreast is:	Part of a woman's chest.
A Camisole:	Something to do with religion
The Change:	What you get from a fiver when you buy a paper
Lip Gloss:	A new type of emulsion
PMT:	An evening television programme
Foundation:	The support for a building
Eye Liner:	A new type of insulation
Pan Stick:	Used to turn the fry on the pan
Cleavage:	What a butcher uses for chopping up meat
Hair Extensions:	Not sure but must be something to do with building
Web Page:	A spider's newspaper
Polygon:	A dead Parrot
Minimum:	A small mammy

Offence:	Goes around a garden
Smooth Operator:	When you cross a telephone with an iron
Claustrophobia	A fear of Santa Claus
Wii:	What you do in the toilet
Pork Scratchings:	When you cross a pig with a flee
Karma:	The Mammy's Car
Spa:	Corner shop that opens late
A Smear:	Something bad said about your personality
Clutch bag:	Has to be something to do with a car
Arm Candy:	A handful of sweets
Wedges:	Like chips but thicker
Pedicure:	Medicine for the dog
Botox:	Posh name for your bum
Homeopath:	Walkway around the house
Moisturiser:	Too much rainfall
A Face Mask:	Another word for a balaclava
Psychic:	A sideline kick in football
Stretch Marks:	Tyre marks on the road also known as skid marks
Concealer:	A type of paint to hide DIY errors

Leggins:	Everyone has two, they link the toes to the hips
A Lightbulb Moment:	When you find a bulb in your cupboard
Eating Out:	Picnics
Essential Oil:	A must have engine oil for the car
Genes:	Denim Trousers
A Crown:	A hat worn by a King

What Your Star Sign Says About You

Capricorn: 22nd December – 20th January

You have an ambitious and disciplined approach to life. You can be a little reserved. This makes you vulnerable at times, and you worry that you will choose the wrong man!

Aquarius: 21st January – 19th February

You are a great communicator Aquarius. You demand respect and trust from friends/partner, can be a bit off-putting. You are talented with multiple interests.

Pisces: 20th February – 20th March

You Pisces are a sensual, intuitive gal with a great sense of humour. You can however be a bit of a dreamer and watch that temper, it could get you into hot water.

Aries: 21st March – 20th April

Ms Independent. You love life and your wide smile is your best feature. You are brave and fearless in all your endeavors. Proud of your figure though!

Taurus: 21st April – 21st May

Fashion conscious! You love expensive clothes and accessories. You can be a little reserved. Good at analyzing situations quickly and making the correct judgments.

Gemini: 22nd May – 21st June

The optimist of the Zodiac. Always looking to improve things around you, problem being this can be annoying to others. You like intelligent men and enjoy having good conversations with them.

Cancer: 22nd June – 23rd July

An introvert Cancer. You don't like aggression or a casual approach to relationships.
Security is important to you. Family and romance means a lot and this often sees you engaging in self – sacrifice.

Leo: 24th July – 23rd August

You like praise Ms Leo and can be seen to be a little vain. You are one of the most beautiful of the signs. Fair and generous in your outlook you are not afraid to speak out.

Virgo: 24th August – 23rd September

All work and no play Virgo. Angelic in appearance you are a smart lady. Impeccably groomed you can be charming if a little reserved in expressing your feelings.

Libra: 24th September – 23rd October

The trend setter of the Zodiac. Artistic in nature you try to improve your surroundings to suit your refined tasted. With a fair and balanced outlook you give sound, good advice.

Scorpio: 24th October – 22nd November

You Ms Scorpio is a talented lady, but you use this to get your own way at times. Sincere in your dealings and don't like lies. Scorpion's are usually tall and well built.

Sagittarius: 23rd November – 21st December

Generous to a fault with a great sense of humour, makes you Ms. Popular of the Zodiac. You value your freedom and find it hard to commit to a certain person or career.

A Dumb Girl's Guide to a successful Relationship:

After years of analysis as to why men and women are different and still no closer to finding a formula which would help us all get along, the following guidelines may add to a harmonious relationship. Remember Girls Love is a Strange but Wonderful thing.

Have fun "yall"
Attend to your boyfriend. Inattention marks disinterest and signifies that what he is saying is not worth listening to.

Consult him on everything, from the cut of meat you buy for his dinner to the colour of blouse you should wear. Constant consultation communicates respect.

Gaze lovingly at him when he addresses you and nod your agreement to what he proposes.

Say as little about yourself, your family and your friends as possible, this allows him to talk as much as he wants about his.

Don't try to be wiser or more knowledgeable than him, this will boost his ego and self esteem.

Never interrupt him, sit or stand still when he is speaking so as not to cause him to lose his train of thought.

Hang on his every word.

Don't talk too long or too frequently as this will cut in to his time.

Lavish him with complements and praise.

Buy him expensive toys for his birthday and Christmas.

Do not have unrealistic expectations of him such as cleaning up after himself or washing the dishes.

Allow him to spend recklessly while you scrimp and save.

Don't ever complain if he's late home or stays out all night. This would be seen as questioning his judgment. You accept that he will always act in your best interest.

Gals is Santa Male or Female?
Santa must be female'cos:

No man could organize such a huge social event as this.

A man would find the commitment of every year too much.

Men would not wear a red and white suit with knee high black boots.

Men would never answer all those Dear Santa letters.

A man would not come down the chimney they would use the more convenient option of the back door

Men do not pack bags/sacks sensibly.

A man would leave getting the presents 'till the last minute. By then all the good ones would be gone. Children everywhere would end up getting the same things.

Going from house to house most men would not ask for directions so would end up getting lost and arriving late.

Men would not cope well with the stress of it all!

Do you agree gals?

Seasonal Smiles:

Why did the child spell Christmas N-O-E?
Because the teacher said No L

Why is Santa so jolly?
'Cos he knows where all the naughty girls live

Why is Christmas like a working day for some?
They do all the work while the fat man in the suit gets all the credit.

What sort of flour does Mrs. Claus use in her mince pies?
Elf-raising.

What is in your future on Christmas Eve that will be in your past on Christmas day?
Your Christmas presents.

A sign outside Santa's Grotto: All children must be accompanied by money or Daddy.

What did the big cracker say to the little cracker?
My pop is louder then yours.

Two young boys are talking after Christmas;

1st boy: We had Grannie and Grandad for Christmas dinner.
2nd boy: What – no turkey?

Seasonal Smilies

What did Adam say on the day before Christmas?
It's Christmas, Eve.

****

How do you know Santa has to be a man?
No woman is going to wear the same outfit year after year.

****

What have Christmas trees and bad knitters got in common?
They both drop their needles.

****

Mum, can I have a puppy for Christmas? six year old Josh asked
"No love" his Mum replied you can have turkey like everybody else.

****

What is red and white and goes oh-oh-oh?
Santa Claus going backwards.

****

How is a flag like Santa?
They both hang out at the pole.

****

What do you get if Santa goes down a chimney when there is a fire on?
Crisp Cringle.

****

What do you get when you cross a snowman with a vampire?
Frostbite.

Two young boys were staying with their grandparents the week-end before Christmas.

What are you doing? Wayne asked his brother when he found him kneeling on his bed with his hands clasped tightly together.

"I'm praying for a Wii".   Peter aged eight called out excitedly.

Stop shouting, the older one said, "God isn't deaf".

"I know", his brother answered.   "But Granny is".

****

A young girl complained to the teacher after the school holidays that Santa hadn't brought her what she had asked for.

"Oh dear", the teacher said sympathetically.   "What did you ask for?"
"A baby", the little girl replied.

****

What's the difference between Santa and a hot dog?
Santa wears a suit, a hot dog pants only.

****

What do you call a blind reindeer?
No eye dear.

****

What does Santa put in his reindeer on frosty mornings?
Santy-Freeze.

****

Howlers:

The bride wore white and carried a fresh bucket.

****

Her husband the electrician was a real bright spark if ever there was one.

****

There are eleven letters in the alphabet, t,h,and e, that's three plus a, l, p, h, a, b, e and t.

****

The woman explained that her wardrobe was packed with nothing to wear.

****

A sign in a café declared 'please do not touch the food".

****

Sign at a seaside, "No butts on sand".

****

Female mid forties would like to meet mature mare (male) for stable relationship.

****

She felt better after rusting (resting) on the couch for a couple of hours.

****

It's pretty purple loaves (leaves) sweat in the sun.

****

In this wife (life) I'm a man. In my next wife (life) I'd like to be a robot.

****

I was thirteen weeks pregnant when I had my first scam (scan)

You're churning up inside, wondering about whether or not you'll hit it off but these are only first-rate (date) nerves.

Tom and Renee had been fed (wed) for nearly forty tears.

And
The celebrations went on until the early hours, bonfires blazed and the champagne glowed (flowed).

Did you ever meet a dummy (yummy) mummy gals?

Annie's friends said she was having a mid-wife (life) crisis 'cos she would only date younger men. They wished she would meet a more premature (mature) man.

Gals were asked to perfect their lout (pout) – Create a lout (pout) that is full, shiny and perfect.

An older lady complained to her doctor that she couldn't see anything 'cos her vision was furry (blurry). While another struggled financially 'cos she had been tipped (ripped) off!

Believe it or not gals!

****

Free to good home, Pomeranian cross dog, good with children and other dogs.

****

She'd had a throbbing headache all day so she took two parachutes and had an early night.

****

A Recipe:

(B) Eat two eggs in a bowl and mix in the sugar.
Peace (place) under a pre-heated grill.

****

Looking for love, Advert -
Attractive single lady, enjoys most things in life w.l.t.m. someone special

****

The blue skirt she bought for eighty euro two months ago was now too tight. "What a waist", she wailed.

****

"His idea of a dirty week-end", Harriet cackled to Maisie "is a wet week-end on his uncle's farm milking cows rather than a pamper week-end in a posh hotel".

****

Shopping List:

6 egos (eggs)
Auntie ageing cream
Grave juice
Self-raising floor
Packet of streaky rashes
Sag and onion stuffing
BBQ Chicken sings (wings)

Lightning Source UK Ltd.
Milton Keynes UK
UKOW050235160312

189057UK00001B/115/P